Gramma.
Tongue T

THAT BLOKE'S BACK BRAKE-BLOCK BROKE

Try repeating this sentence in quick succession without faltering or stuttering, and don't be surprised to see your tongue twisted in the process!

Armed with this fabulous collection of nearly a thousand tongue-twisters, enliven a party, or confuse your friends, or surprise your seniors, and get any tongue in the world truly twisted!

Pick your pick from a string of pepper-pickers, seashell- sellers, woodchucking-woodchuckers, knick-knack knitters, etc, that will put the dexterity of your lips and tongue to the test.

Say this sharply, say this sweetly,
Say this shortly, say this softly.
Say this sixteen times in succession.

BOOKS IN ENGLISH LANGUAGE LEARNING SERIES

Grammer Matters

Common Errors in English

Dictionary for Misspellers

Idioms

Quotations

Proverbs

Riddles

Tongue Twisters

The Complete Guide to

Business Letters

Effective English Writing

Essays for Competitive Examinations

Functional Writing in English

Modern Essays

Paragraph to Essay Writing

Prose Compositions

Résumé Writing

Letters for Social Interaction

Enrich your Grammar

Antonyms

Current Words and Phrases

Prepositions

Synonyms

Word Perfect

Word Power

Word to Paragraph

Words and Their Usages

Word Origins

Communications Skills

The Power of Spoken English (with 2 audio CDs)

Speaking and Writing in English

Dynamic Reading Skills

Effective Communication

English Conversation Practice

How to Develop Profitable Listening Skills

How to Increase Your Reading Speed

How to Listen Better

How to Read Effectively and Efficiently

How to Resolve Conflicts

Grammar Matters
Tongue Twisters

Gratian Vas

Sterling Paperback

STERLING PAPERBACKS
An imprint of
Sterling Publishers (P) Ltd.
A-59, Okhla Industrial Area, Phase-II,
New Delhi-110020.
Tel: 26387070, 26386209; Fax: 91-11-26383788
E-mail: sterlingpublishers@airtelbroadband.in
ghai@nde.vsnl.net.in
www.sterlingpublishers.com

Tongue Twisters
© 2006, Sterling Publishers Pvt. Ltd., New Delhi-110020
ISBN 978-81-207-1780-0
Reprint 2007, 2008

Printed and Published by Sterling Publishers Pvt. Ltd., New Delhi-110 020.

PREFACE

Can you say each of the following five times in quick succession without faltering or stuttering?

The crow flew over the river
With a raw lump of liver

OR

A fly flew past Flo's flat,
And a fly flew past fat Flo,
Is the fly that flew past fat Flo,
The same fly that flew past Flo's flat?

Ah! Not as simple as you thought. No big surprise if you've actually got your tongue twisted in the process!

A tongue-twister is a word, phrase or sentence which is difficult to utter rapidly due to the repetition of similar sounds or alliteration of the consonants.

The Sterling Book of Tongue-Twisters has nearly 1,000 tongue-twisters about pepper-pickers, seashell-sellers and woodchucking woodchuckers that will put the dexterity of your lips and tongue to the test and presumably help you pronounce them clearly.

Armed with this fabulous, alphabetically arranged collection you can confuse your friends, surprise your parents, tease your teachers and get any tongue in the world truly twisted!

Gratian Vas

A big beadle placed a body in a big black bag.

☆   ☆   ☆

A black backed bath-brush.

☆   ☆   ☆

A black spot on the black back of a black-spotted haddock.

☆   ☆   ☆

A box of biscuits,
A box of mixed biscuits,
And a biscuit mixer.

☆   ☆   ☆

A canner exceedingly canny,
One day remarked to his granny:
'A canner can can
Anything that he can,
But a canner can't can a can, can he?'

☆   ☆   ☆

A clean copper coal scuttle.

☆   ☆   ☆

A coster carried crates of cabbages across a crooked court.

A clipper shipped several clipped sheep.
Were these clipped sheep the clipper ship's
   sheep?
Or just clipped sheep shipped on a clipper's
   ship?

☆   ☆   ☆

A cricket critic cricked his neck at a critical
cricket match.

☆   ☆   ☆

A cunning and clever and capricious captain
commanded several centurions in Capricorn.

☆   ☆   ☆

A dozen double damask dinner napkins.

☆   ☆   ☆

A dozen droopy damsels dawdled despondently
   down the docks.

☆   ☆   ☆

A fat-thighed freak fries thick steak.

☆   ☆   ☆

A fly flew past Flo's flat,
And a fly flew past fat Flo.
Is the fly that flew past fat Flo,
The same fly that flew past Flo's flat?

☆   ☆   ☆

A frightened thief from Farnham fought his way from the floodlit fireworks factory.

☆ ☆ ☆

A gaggle of geese gobbled gluttonously.

☆ ☆ ☆

A Glasgow glazier's glorious gleaming green glass gasglobes.

☆ ☆ ☆

A gleam glimmered in the glen, glowing ghostly in the gloaming.

☆ ☆ ☆

A glowing gleam glowing green.

☆ ☆ ☆

Agnes looked askance at Horace's tie which was awry and at Hilda's skirt all askew.

☆ ☆ ☆

A hundredweight of Hopwort will make an awful lot of beer or a lot of awful beer.

☆ ☆ ☆

A knapsack strap.

☆ ☆ ☆

A laurel-crowned clown.

A jester
From Leicester
Went to see
Esther,
But as Esther
Was taking her
Siesta,
The jester from
Leicester
Didn't see
Esther.

☆   ☆   ☆

Albert had a habit of eating hot halibut.

☆   ☆   ☆

Alex from Albany ambled around Alhambra.

☆   ☆   ☆

A lively young fisher named Fischer.
Fished for fish from the edge of a fissure.
A fish with a grin pulled the fisherman in!
Now they're fishing the fissure
For Fischer.

☆   ☆   ☆

A lovely large labrador licked Linda lovingly.

☆   ☆   ☆

Although degraded, Drake denied his dereliction
of duty.

All I want is a proper cup of coffee
Made in a proper copper coffee pot.
You can believe it or not,
But I just want a cup of coffee
In a proper coffee pot.
Tin coffee pots
Or iron coffee pots
Are no use to me.
If I can't have a proper cup of coffee,
In a proper copper coffee pot,
I'll have a cup of tea!

☆   ☆   ☆

A lump of red leather, a red leather lump.

☆   ☆   ☆

Amanda Millicent McGuire amended a messy
manuscript with muddled emendations.

☆   ☆   ☆

A man from Grantham broke a big
chrysanthemum, mum.

☆   ☆   ☆

A maid with a duster
Made a furious bluster
Dusting a bust in the hall.
When the bust it was dusted
The bust it was busted,
The bust it was dust,
That's all

Am I and Amy aiming anaemic anemones on my many enemies?

☆   ☆   ☆

Amidst the mists and coldest frosts,
With barest wrists and stoutest boasts,
He thrusts his fists against the posts,
But still insists he sees the ghosts.

☆   ☆   ☆

Amazing Annie Ashford asks for four frightening flashes.

☆   ☆   ☆

A monk's monkey mounted a monastery wall munching mashed melon and melted macaroni.

☆   ☆   ☆

An artist went to sea to see what he could see at sea to draw, but all the artist saw at sea was what we always see at sea — sea, see?

☆   ☆   ☆

And ere the ear had heard,
Her heart had heard.

☆   ☆   ☆

An elevator on Everest: an Everest elevator.

☆   ☆   ☆

A new snipped sixpence snipped all round.

Andrew Airpump asked his Aunt her ailment.
Did Andrew Airpump ask his Aunt her ailment?
If Andrew Airpump asked his Aunt her ailment,
What was the ailment of Andrew Airpump's
Aunt?

☆　　☆　　☆

Angelina oiled the hinges on her oil engine with
oil-engine oil.

☆　　☆　　☆

A nice moose married a nice mouse.

☆　　☆　　☆

An oyster met an oyster and they were oysters
two;
Two oysters met two oysters and they were
oysters too;
Four oysters met a pint of milk and they were
oyster stew!

☆　　☆　　☆

Anthea and Andy ate acid apples accidentally.

☆　　☆　　☆

Anthony Ackroyd had adenoids, acne and
hammer-toe.

☆　　☆　　☆

Anxious Annie ambled awkwardly up to Averil's
oven.

Any noise annoys an oyster, but a noisy noise annoys an oyster most.

☆   ☆   ☆

A plain pinewood police van, privately packed with protesting prisoners, plies periodically to Parkhurst prison.

☆   ☆   ☆

A plethora of pigeons plied between the pillars of the pier.

☆   ☆   ☆

A poor pauper paused on purpose to pawn a porpoise.

☆   ☆   ☆

A portion of plum pudding was put before Peter Pratt who promptly put it down his pudding-chute.

☆   ☆   ☆

A purely rural duel truly plural is better than a purely plural duel truly rural.

☆   ☆   ☆

A queer quick questioning quiz.

☆   ☆   ☆

Architectural assets assist accurate accounting.

Are there any ancient archeologists abroad agreeable to grant access?

☆   ☆   ☆

Are you copper-bottoming 'em, my man?'
'No, I'm aluminiuming 'em, Ma'am!'

☆   ☆   ☆

A roving raven on the roofing—raving!

☆   ☆   ☆

Artful Alex aimed eight awful arrows.

☆   ☆   ☆

A rural ruler should be truly rural and recognise rural raillery.

☆   ☆   ☆

A selfish shellfish smelt a stalefish.
If the stale fish was a smelt
Then the selfish shellfish smelt a smelt.

☆   ☆   ☆

A shadow sometimes settled on the settle where Sheila sat her Suluki.

☆   ☆   ☆

A ship saileth south soon.

☆   ☆   ☆

A shifty shark seeling snake skin slippers.

A shooting suit that's suitable for shooting,
Should be made of a suiting that is suitable.
If not made of a suiting that is suitable,
Then that shooting suit's not suitable for
   shooting!

☆   ☆   ☆

A shy little she said 'Shoo!'
To a fly and a flea in a flue.

☆   ☆   ☆

A sick sparrow sang six sad spring songs
sitting sheltering under a squat shrub.

☆   ☆   ☆

A snakebite is a serious setback and some
serum should be sought straightaway.

☆   ☆   ☆

As I was going past Esau's yard, I saw a man
sawing and of all the sawers I ever saw I never
saw a saw saw like that saw sawed!

☆   ☆   ☆

A sloven in a shawl shovelled soft snow slowly.

☆   ☆   ☆

As the roaring rocket rose, the restless roosters
rollicked.

☆   ☆   ☆

As I went into the garden,
  I saw five brave maids
Sitting on five broad beds
  Braiding broad braids.
I said to these five brave maids
  Sitting on five broad beds
Braiding broad braids,
  'Braid broad braids, brave maids.'

☆   ☆   ☆

A sudden sibilant whisper shouldn't make one shudder, should it?

☆   ☆   ☆

A tall eastern girl named Short long loved a big Mr. Little. But Little, thinking little of Short, loved a little lass named Long. To belittle Long, Short announced she would marry Little before long. This caused Little shortly to marry Long. To make a long story short, did tall Short love big Little less because Little loved little Long more?

☆   ☆   ☆

A thousand freckles was a feature of his face.

☆   ☆   ☆

A thousand theatres thunder with applause.

☆   ☆   ☆

A tidy tiger tied a tie tighter to tidy her tiny tail.

A tooter who tooted a flute
Tried to tutor two tooters to toot.
Said the two to their tutor,
'Is it harder to toot or
To tutor two tutors to toot?'

☆　　☆　☆

A tree toad loved a she-toad
That lived up in a tree.
She was a three-toed tree toad,
But a two-toed toad was he.

☆　☆　☆

A truly rural frugal ruler's mural.

☆　☆　☆

At present you can't marry a peasant however
pleasant the peasant may be.

☆　☆　☆

A twister of twists once twisted a twist
And the twist that he twisted was a three-
    twisted twist.
Now in twisting this twist, if a twist should
    untwist.
The twist that untwisted would untwist the
    twist.

☆　☆　☆

A white witch watched a woebegone walrus
winding white wool.

A wine van ran through the vine.

☆　　☆　　☆

Auntie Annie asked everybody if anybody was anti-aunties.
If anybody is anti-aunties, which auntie is anybody anti?

☆　　☆　　☆

Babbling Bert blamed Bess.

☆　　☆　　☆

Babbling Brain blames Bertha.

☆　　☆　　☆

Bandy-legged Borachio Mustachio Whiskerifustious, the bald and brave Bombandino of Baghdad, helped Abomilique Bluebeard Bashaw of Babelmandel to beat down an abominable bumblebee at Balsora!

☆　　☆　　☆

Barry Berry buries Barry's beret.

☆　　☆　　☆

Bees hoard heaps of honey in hives.

Barry Broadbread belted out the 'Bartered Bride' ballad bawdily.

☆   ☆   ☆

Battling Bill bullied the blustering brigand beside the bunker.

☆   ☆   ☆

Beautiful babbling brooks bubble between blossoming banks.

☆   ☆   ☆

Beautiful Bonnie Bliss blows blissfully beautiful bubbles.

☆   ☆   ☆

Benny Butler bought bitter butter in a brass bell but broke it.

☆   ☆   ☆

Bert brought bought bricks.

☆   ☆   ☆

Beryl burned the brown bread badly.

☆   ☆   ☆

Better batter. Bitter butter.

☆   ☆   ☆

Big Billy has a big belly and is a big bully.

Betty Batter had some butter,
'But', she said, 'this butter's bitter.
If I bake this bitter butter,
It would make my batter bitter.'

☆   ☆   ☆

Betty beat a bit of butter to make a better batter.

☆   ☆   ☆

Betty Bother bathed in bathsuds with a bathbun sponge.

☆   ☆   ☆

Betty Botter battered batter better than Betty Bitter buttered butter.

☆   ☆   ☆

Betty Brown blinked and brandished the big broom at the beast.

☆   ☆   ☆

Big black bluebottles buzzed boisterously below Billy's nose.

☆   ☆   ☆

Big Bill Billiken blew bursting bubbles by billions.

☆   ☆   ☆

Big brown bulb-bowls.

Big brown bumblebees were buried beside the bulbs in Bobby Brook's bulb bowls, basket and boxes.

☆   ☆   ☆

Big bugs, bed bugs.

☆   ☆   ☆

Bill Bodger brought Brian a bit of boiled bacon in a brown bag.

☆   ☆   ☆

Billy's big blue badly bleeding blister.

☆   ☆   ☆

Billy Bolton buttoned his bright brown boots and blue coat before breakfast began.

☆   ☆   ☆

Black bug's blood.

☆   ☆   ☆

Black dog danced on the barn floor barefoot.

☆   ☆   ☆

Blame the big bleak black book.

☆   ☆   ☆

Blissful Brenda blithely backing Britain.

☆   ☆   ☆

Blonde Blodwin Blossom blushes bashfully.

☆ ☆ ☆

Blodwin brought back black bric-a-brac.

☆ ☆ ☆

Bluebottle's bottle's blue.

☆ ☆ ☆

Bold Bob and brave Bea bought a billion beavers back from Boston.

☆ ☆ ☆

Brenda bites Bourbon biscuits briskly.

☆ ☆ ☆

Brenda Blenkiron braised a box of British bloaters.

☆ ☆ ☆

Brian blatantly boasted and bragged of his blank verse and his black pudding.

☆ ☆ ☆

Bright blows the broom on the brook's bare brown banks.

☆ ☆ ☆

Bring back bright brand—new British brushes from breezy Bridlington.

Bring back the Brighton Bells.

☆   ☆   ☆

British 'Back Britain' badges and brooches.

☆   ☆   ☆

Broad beamed Bertha breathes bad breath.

☆   ☆   ☆

Buy Bridges' British breeches!

☆   ☆   ☆

Cameron came careering round the corner, completing his crazy career by crashing into the crypt.

☆   ☆   ☆

Can an actor act at Action in an action packed epic?
If an actor can't act at Action in an action packed epic,
Where can an actor act?

☆   ☆   ☆

Can Carol croon carols?

Can clever cooks cook clocks, or should cooks not cook clocks?

☆   ☆   ☆

Can Colin climb chimney stacks carefully?

☆   ☆   ☆

Can consuming cold cod cutlets cause corns?

☆   ☆   ☆

Can Corky really cook cabbage chips, Kathy?

☆   ☆   ☆

Can Kelly catch Clara before she cuts the chintz curtains up?

☆   ☆   ☆

Can Kenneth come crab-catching in Cleethorpes, Chloe?

☆   ☆   ☆

Can Kitty cuddle Clara's kitten?

☆   ☆   ☆

Can you imagine, an imaginary menagerie manager imagining managing an imaginery menagerie?

☆   ☆   ☆

Carly Coo-Coo cooked cuckoos in cold custard.

Can you imagine the hindrance when the Hindu
and the Israeli indulged in inane histrionics on
the history of the hierarchy in India?

☆   ☆   ☆

Cardinal Crowbridge's cracks creased the
crowded congregation.

☆   ☆   ☆

Cautious Carol choked carelessly on a chunk of
chocolate.

☆   ☆   ☆

Charlie chooses cheese and cherries.

☆   ☆   ☆

Cheeky Charlie Ching plays Chinese Checkers
much better than Marjoria Wong plays mahjong.

☆   ☆   ☆

'Cheap cheep', chirped the cheery chaffinch.

☆   ☆   ☆

Cheerful Chan the
Chinaman sips sister
Celia's sherry.

☆   ☆   ☆

Cheerful Charles chose cherry chocolates for
Cheri.

Cheerful children chant charming tunes.

☆   ☆   ☆

Cheryl's chilly cheap chip shop sells Cheryl's cheap chips.

☆   ☆   ☆

Cherry Chocolate Cups.

☆   ☆   ☆

Chief Sheik, sheep section.

☆   ☆   ☆

Chimes challenged the changing year.

☆   ☆   ☆

Chloe was coquettish and considerate and skilfully contemporary, except when she had the collywobbles.

☆   ☆   ☆

Chris, unfurl your kiss-curl!

☆   ☆   ☆

Christian Christabel's Christmas crackers.

☆   ☆   ☆

Christmas crackers create a cracking Christmas.

☆   ☆   ☆

Coffee chocolate toffee apples.

Claire collected the cabbages, carrots, courgettes and macaroni cheese.

☆   ☆   ☆

Clearly the clause in Klaus's contract causes Klaus confusion.

☆   ☆   ☆

Clever Carlton constructed coal carts out of crates.

☆   ☆   ☆

Clever Clifford clapped conjurer Clive's clever tricks.

☆   ☆   ☆

Cliff Cross crossed the criss-cross crossing.
The criss-cross crossing Cliff Cross crossed.
When Cliff Cross crossed the criss-cross crossing.
Where's the criss-cross crossing Cliff Cross crossed?

☆   ☆   ☆

Cold cream clings in clottish clods.

☆   ☆   ☆

Coline cuddled Cora in the car and caught his camera on the clutch.

☆   ☆   ☆

Cook cooked a cup of cold creamy custard.

☆　　☆　　☆

Cool pools are foolproof pools for washing wool.

☆　　☆　　☆

Cornish clotted cream cartons.

☆　　☆　　☆

Could a clever carpenter chisel cedar coat racks?

☆　　☆　　☆

Could Queenie's callers come quietly, Clarence?

☆　　☆　　☆

Cows graze in droves on grass which grows in grooves on groves.

☆　　☆　　☆

Crazy Claude catches crawling crabs.

☆　　☆　　☆

Crazy cooks cut chunky chips for cheeky chaps.

☆　　☆　　☆

'Crikey!' cried Chris, 'can't you keep the gates clear of clutter and keep the kids quiet?'

Crime cuts out crime.

☆   ☆   ☆

Cruel cannibals carelessly cooked the quaking cricketer from Chelmsford.

☆   ☆   ☆

Crunch crispy crisps quickly.

☆   ☆   ☆

Crusts and crumbs and crunchy cake with clotted cream and custard and Christmas crackers.

☆   ☆   ☆

Curious quiet calm.

☆   ☆   ☆

Curly Colin Cluster clips chrysanthemum clumps carelessly.
If curly Colin Cluster carelessly clips chrysanthemum clumps,
Where are the chrysanthemum clumps curly Colin Cluster carelessly clips?

☆   ☆   ☆

Cut Caroline's cauliflower and catch crawling crabs, Cynthia.

☆   ☆   ☆

Cuthbert was caught coughing in his coffin.

Cynthia couldn't clean the cloisters: the cloisters were cloying and claustrophobic.

☆ ☆ ☆

Daring Dan dashed dizzily down the dale doing damaging deeds as he went.

☆ ☆ ☆

Daring Dora dashed dizzily down the doctors' driveway.

☆ ☆ ☆

Darling Diana danced delightfully during December's dances.

☆ ☆ ☆

Dashing Daniel defied David to deliver Dora from the dawning danger.

☆ ☆ ☆

Dauntless Doris Davis does a dozen daring dives daily.

☆ ☆ ☆

Deeply dreadful dreams.

Deirdre was dreadfully downhearted and depressed when she found she was deplorably disorientated.

☆   ☆   ☆

Demented divers drive the dolphins down to the depths of the sea.

☆   ☆   ☆

Did Diddy David dawdle down the dale, or did Dale dawdle down to Diddy David's.

☆   ☆   ☆

Did Monty make money madly in Monte Carlo, or did Monte Carlo make money out of Monty, Mother?

☆   ☆   ☆

Did the Dean drink dandelion wine?

☆   ☆   ☆

Diggory Dog dug deep deep dug outs down which he dived to dig up bones.

☆   ☆   ☆

Diligence dismisseth despondency.

☆   ☆   ☆

Dimpled Diana danced in dainty dimity down the dunes.

Do breath tests test breath?
Yes, that's the best of a breath test.
So the best breath stands the breath test best!

☆   ☆   ☆

Dodo's dog died of distemper, a disease which does dogs down.

☆   ☆   ☆

Do you stock shorts socks with spots in your shop?
Does Dora adore a doorknob, or does a door not adore Dora?

☆   ☆   ☆

Don had doubts and didn't dare to anything to endanger the duenna.

☆   ☆   ☆

Don't miss the maths master's messages.

☆   ☆   ☆

Don't run along the wrong lane.

☆   ☆   ☆

Dopey Denis dances dangerously in Denmark.

☆   ☆   ☆

Dorothy dawdled and doodled in a daydream as she dusted down the dresser in the drawing room.

Double bubble gum bubbles double!

☆   ☆   ☆

Double-o-Seven was dishevelled and disillusioned and determined to discontinue his distorted distractions.

☆   ☆   ☆

Down the slippery slide they slid
Sitting slightly sideways;
Slipping swiftly see them skid
On holidays and Fridays.

☆   ☆   ☆

Dressed in drip-dry drawers.

☆   ☆   ☆

Eat Esther's early Easter eggs, Edgar.

☆   ☆   ☆

Educated Eliza elephant enjoys everything elegant.

☆   ☆   ☆

Eight ethereal arch-angles each had heavenly halos.

Eight grey geese gazing gaily into Greece.

☆   ☆   ☆

Eight hefty hecklers harangued the orator who had to hurry hastily from the hall.

☆   ☆   ☆

Elevating eleven elephants.

☆   ☆   ☆

Eleven elves in Hell.

☆   ☆   ☆

Eli eats the eels from Ealing.

☆   ☆   ☆

Elizabeth lisps lengthy lessons.

☆   ☆   ☆

Evan Ewan's eaten eighteen eggs.

☆   ☆   ☆

Even Stephen's even oven's on.

☆   ☆   ☆

Enlightened Elizabeth eloped in earnest with Ernest.

☆   ☆   ☆

Evil Edna helped herself to eleven cups of elevenses.

☆   ☆   ☆

Eugene endeavoured to play the euphonium and usually hushed the audience who ushered him from the room.

☆   ☆   ☆

Famous friezes figures fabulously.

☆   ☆   ☆

Fancy Fanny Franks feeling funny about
Fred Ferraby's fishing flies, for
Fred Ferraby fishes with flies to flying fishes.

☆   ☆   ☆

Fanny Fetter found a fan
A fan found Fanny Fetter,
But Fanny Fetter lost her fan —
And wept till she felt better.

☆   ☆   ☆

Fanny fumbled, faltered, then fainted.

Fancy Nancy didn't fancy doing fancy work.
But Fancy Nancy's fancy aunty did fancy
Fancy Nancy doing fancy work!

☆   ☆   ☆

Fearless Frank flew fast flights to Frankfurt.

☆   ☆   ☆

Farmer Fresshitt's fresh farm eggs fry furiously
in Farmer Fresshitt's frying pan.

☆   ☆   ☆

Fearless Frank following in Fanallioni's feuding
family's footsteps.

☆   ☆   ☆

Fetch fifty-five foils.

☆   ☆   ☆

Figs form fine fancy fare.

☆   ☆   ☆

Fiona felt fraught at Freddie's fulsome flattery
and frankly thought it rather foolish.

☆   ☆   ☆

Fiona felt the French film was fatuous and
flashy.

☆   ☆   ☆

Fiona Fly flew faster than a fine flying flea.

Five fashionable females flying to France for fresh French fashions.

☆   ☆   ☆

Five flashy flappers
Flitting forth fleetingly
Found four flighty flappers
Flirting flippantly.

☆   ☆   ☆

Five frantic fat frogs fled from fifty fierce fishes.

☆   ☆   ☆

Five French friars fanning a fainted flea.

☆   ☆   ☆

Flora's fan fluttered feebly and her fine fingers fidgeted.

☆   ☆   ☆

Flee from fog to fight 'flu fast.

☆   ☆   ☆

Flocking shoppers shopping.

☆   ☆   ☆

Florence Freeman fell forward and frightened her father frightfully.

☆   ☆   ☆

For four far furriers further forward.

☆   ☆   ☆

Forty fat farmers fought over a field of fine fresh fodder.

☆   ☆   ☆

Four famous fisherman found for flounders—flippers flapping furiously—faithfully following four floppy female flatfish.

☆   ☆   ☆

Four famished Finlanders frying flying fish.

☆   ☆   ☆

Four fat friars frying fat fish.

☆   ☆   ☆

Four fat dogs frying fritters and fiddling ferociously.

☆   ☆   ☆

Four fat fish fanned flickering flames.

☆   ☆   ☆

Francis Fowler's father fried five floundering flounders for Francis Fowler's father's father.

☆   ☆   ☆

Freckled-faced Florence frowned furiously.

Francis fries fresh fish fillets for Frederick.
Frederick fillets four fresh fish for Francis' fried
fillets.

☆   ☆   ☆

Freddie's father is fastidious, fretful and
inflexible.

☆   ☆   ☆

Fresh-fried fowl flesh.

☆   ☆   ☆

Frisky Felix feeds on freshly fried fishes.

☆   ☆   ☆

Gaily gathered the gleaners the glossy golden
grain and garnered it gladly in Granny's great
granary in Godfrey's green glassy glen.

☆   ☆   ☆

Gay gallants gambolling on the green grass.

☆   ☆   ☆

Gay Gladys glanced bravely at grave Greta and
glided glitteringly past guilty Grace at the glorious
garden gala.

Gay Gordon Grassington goes eating grass on Whitsuntide.

☆   ☆   ☆

Gaze on the grey gay brigade.

☆   ☆   ☆

George Gibbs grabs crabs,
Crabs George Gibbs grabs,
If George Gibbs grabs crabs,
Where are the crabs George Gibbs grabs?

☆   ☆   ☆

'Gee whiz, show biz,' said Miss Dixie Fizz.

☆   ☆   ☆

Gig-whip, gig-whip, gig-whip.

☆   ☆   ☆

Give George Green gloves and gleaming galoshes.

☆   ☆   ☆

Gladys' glamorous grannie grew more and more garrulous.

☆   ☆   ☆

Gloria Groot glued a groat to Gregory's goat.

☆   ☆   ☆

Glorious Gwendoline gave Gloria gladiolis.

'Gone, gone, gone, gone, gone', groaned the grumpy greengrocer.

☆   ☆   ☆

Good, better, best,
Never let it rest
Till your good is better,
And your better best.

☆   ☆   ☆

Good blue blood, bad black blood.

☆   ☆   ☆

Good gardeners grow great gherkins.

☆   ☆   ☆

'Goodbye, Gertie,' gushed Gussie.
'Goodbye, Gussie,' gushed Gertie.

☆   ☆   ☆

Good Goodie Twoshoes took two shoes to the Goodie Shoeshines shoe shop.

☆   ☆   ☆

Goofy gophers gobble goodies gladly.

☆   ☆   ☆

Gormless Gertie grabbed great gladioli.

☆   ☆   ☆

Gracious Glenda gladly glued Gordon's gumstick.

Grace's grey-green gloves glided gracefully to the ground.

☆　　　☆　　　☆

Granny's grey goose greedily gobbled golden grain in Graham's gabled granary.

☆　　　☆　　　☆

Granny Grumpkins grumbled gravely as Gavin gobble goose greedily.

☆　　　☆　　　☆

Great crates create great craters.

☆　　　☆　　　☆

Great Gladys grinned gladly.

☆　　　☆　　　☆

Great green gooseberries growing.

☆　　　☆　　　☆

Greek grapes.

☆　　　☆　　　☆

Green greengages grow in green greengage trees.

☆　　　☆　　　☆

Greta Grubshore grabbed Gordon Godwin with gratitude.

Grinning Gregory grunts graciously.

☆　　　☆　　　☆

Groovy gravy, baby!

☆　　　☆　　　☆

Gyles just jostled James.

☆　　　☆　　　☆

Hand on heart the hypochondriac stipulated the hypothesis that hysterical hyperbole needed anti-histamines.

☆　　　☆　　　☆

Handy Andy's got his Sunday undies on!

☆　　　☆　　　☆

'Hark, an aardvark.'
Mark barked for a lark.

☆　　　☆　　　☆

Harold Aitch calls Aitch Haitch.
If Harold Aitch calls Aitch Haitch,
then Harold Aitch becomes Harold Haitch.

☆　　　☆　　　☆

Has Hannah ever had her hair hennaed?

Has Hilda heard how Helen hurried home?

☆ ☆ ☆

Hath Hazel asthma?

☆ ☆ ☆

'Have you got the knack of the new knapsack strap, Nat?'

☆ ☆ ☆

'Have you prepared the gooseberries, Mary?'
'No, I'm just topping and bottoming them, Ma' am.'

☆ ☆ ☆

Heather was hoping to hop to Tahiti to hack a hibiscus to hand on her hat.

☆ ☆ ☆

Heartless Hannah hung hundreds of hammers in her house and hit heads hardly.

☆ ☆ ☆

Heavenly bells ring on high.

☆ ☆ ☆

He had him eat his own hot ham, so his own hot ham he ate.

☆ ☆ ☆

He is literally literary.

Helen has huge hats with enormous hatpins
holding them in her hair.

☆   ☆   ☆

'Help, help,' hurriedly howled the harrassed
Hottentot.

☆   ☆   ☆

He ran from the Indies
To the Andes
In his undies.

☆   ☆   ☆

High roller.
Low roller.
Lower a roller.

☆   ☆   ☆

His beard descending swept his aged breast.

☆   ☆   ☆

His hat hit Horace, so Horace hollered horribly.

☆   ☆   ☆

His shirt soon shrank in the suds.

☆   ☆   ☆

How Harry hates hounding hares.

☆   ☆   ☆

How high his Highness holds his haughty head!

How has Harry hastened so hurriedly to the hunt?

☆　　☆　　☆

How many cans
Can a canner can,
If a canner
Can can cans?
A canner can can
As many cans
As a canner can,
If a canner can
Can cans!

☆　　☆　　☆

How many cuckoos could a good cook cook if a cook could cook cuckoos?

☆　　☆　　☆

How much caramel can a canny cannibal cram into a camel, if a canny cannibal can cram caramel into a camel?

☆　　☆　　☆

Humphrey Hunchbag had a hundred hungry hedgehogs.

☆　　☆　　☆

Hungry Harry's homely uncle.

☆　　☆　　☆

Hungry Henry Hobson hurries home.

Ian's irksome over icy icicles.

☆   ☆   ☆

'I can think of thin things, six thin things, can
you?'
'Yes, I can think of six thin things, and of six
thick things too'.

☆   ☆   ☆

I caught my tongue on a twister,
Cor, what a terrible pain!
What with 'effs' and 'iths' and 'ishes'
It'll never be straight again!

☆   ☆   ☆

I enjoy eggs enormously.

☆   ☆   ☆

Iced ink.
Iced ink.
Ink iced.
Ink iced.

☆   ☆   ☆

I'd rather lather father
Than father lather me.
When father lathers
He lathers rather free.

I do like cheap sea trips, cheap sea trips on ships.

☆   ☆   ☆

If a chicken and a half laid an egg and a half in a day and a half the farmer wouldn't half have a fit and a half.

☆   ☆   ☆

If a chow chews shoes how does he choose which shoes to chew?

☆   ☆   ☆

If a hair net could net hair,
How much hair could a hair net net,
If that hair net could net hair?

☆   ☆   ☆

If a Hottentot taught
  A Hottentot tot,
To talk ere the tot could totter,
  Ought the Hottentot tot
Be taught to say 'ought' or 'naught',
  Or what ought to be taught her?

☆   ☆   ☆

If a shipshape ship shop stocks six shipshape shop-soiled ships,
How many shipshape shop-soiled ships would six shipshape ship shops stocks?

If a top was to sleep in a sleeper,
And the sleeper beneath him went pop,
It's a logical cert that the top would get hurt,
For there's no sleeper that sleeps like a top!

☆   ☆   ☆

If a woodchuck could chuck wood,
How much wood
Would a woodchuck chuck,
If a woodchuck could chuck wood?

☆   ☆   ☆

If Harry hurries, will hairy Henry hand him a
hundred hammers?

☆   ☆   ☆

If neither he sells seashells,
Nor she sells seashells,
Who shall sell seashells?
Shall seashells be sold?

☆   ☆   ☆

If one doctor doctors another doctor,
Does the doctor who doctors the doctor
    Doctor the doctor the way the doctor he is
doctoring doctors?
Or does he doctor the doctor the way the
    doctor who doctors doctors?

☆   ☆   ☆

I go by Blue Goose bus.

If Roland Reynolds rolled a round roll
Round a round room,
Where is the round room in which
Roland Reynolds rolled
A round roll?

☆   ☆   ☆

If the sleeper in a sleeper sleeps, does the sleeper not in the sleeper on the sleeper sleep?

☆   ☆   ☆

If to hoot and to toot a Hottentot tot was taught by a Hottentot tutor, should the tutor get hot if the Hottentot tot hoots and toots at the Hottentot tutor?

☆   ☆   ☆

Ignatius Higginbottam was indignant at the irregular hours which made him irredeemably irritable.

☆   ☆   ☆

'I know you believe you understand what you think I said, but I am not sure you realise that what you heard is not what I meant.'

☆   ☆   ☆

I leaned over the fence to see Eileen Dover's eyes peer over.

☆   ☆   ☆

I'm a critical cricket critic.

I'm anti Auntie.

☆   ☆   ☆

In July, James Junior just jostled Julia.

☆   ☆   ☆

I need not your needles, they're needless to
  me,
For needing needles were needless you see.
But did my neat trousers but need to be kneed,
I then should have need of your needles indeed.

☆   ☆   ☆

Inigo Impey itched for an Indian image.
Did Inigo Impey itch for an Indian image?
If Inigo Impey itched for an Indian image,
Where's the Indian image Inigo Impey itched
for?

☆   ☆   ☆

Innocent Higgins innocently insulted Isabel
Hartley.

☆   ☆   ☆

I saw a butterfly flutter by yesterday.

☆   ☆   ☆

I see seven seagulls soaring southwards silently.
I saw Esau kissing Kate,

☆   ☆   ☆

I saw Esau, he saw me.
And she saw I saw Esau.

☆   ☆   ☆

I shot three shy thrushes.
You shoot three shy thrushes.

☆   ☆   ☆

I snuff shop snuff.
Do you snuff shop snuff?
I snuff enough snuff to stock shop snuff.

☆   ☆   ☆

Is there a pleasant peasant present?

☆   ☆   ☆

Is this Hamlet here, heir to piglet there?

☆   ☆   ☆

It ain't the hunting on the hills that hurts the horses' hooves,
It's the hammer, hammer, hammer on the hard high road.

☆   ☆   ☆

It is imperative to institute immediate investigations into the incident at the hydrodynamics institute.

☆   ☆   ☆

I thought a thought.
But the thought I thought wasn't the thought I thought I thought.
If the thought I thought I thought had been the thought I thought,
I wouldn't have thought so much.

☆   ☆   ☆

I thought he fought a thoroughly fair fight.

☆   ☆   ☆

I was barbarously barbarised by the barbarity of a barbarian barber in a barber's barbarising shop.

☆   ☆   ☆

I was looking back
To see if she was looking back
To see if I was looking back
To see if she was looking back at me.

☆   ☆   ☆

I wish I hadn't washed this wrist watch.
I've washed all the wheels and works.
Oh, how it jumps and jerks.
I wish I hadn't washed this watch's works!

☆   ☆   ☆

I wonder whither the weather will waft the wherry wherein the weather is,
And whether the wherry will weather the weather.

Joan joyously joined jaunty John in jingling jiges.

☆   ☆   ☆

Jock Jones jumped jerkily on Jimmy at the juvenile sports last June.

☆   ☆   ☆

Joe joined Jeffrey and Julian in Jamaica in July not January.

☆   ☆   ☆

Jolly holidays.
Merry jolly days.

☆   ☆   ☆

Jumping Jack jeered a jesting juggler.

☆   ☆   ☆

Jolly Javey jumped joyously juggling jellies at the jubilee.

☆   ☆   ☆

Jonathan jerked on his jerkin for his jogging jaunt and jogged around Jarrow.

☆   ☆   ☆

Joyful Jeanne jeered jokingly as Jamie genuinely jogged.

☆   ☆   ☆

Judy Jordan jumped joyously during Juliana's jubilee jamboree.

☆   ☆   ☆

Keep clean socks in a clean sock stack.

☆   ☆   ☆

Kenneth put the kibosh on the chow when he caught him and kept him in the kennel.

☆   ☆   ☆

Kimbo Kemble kicked his kinsman's kettle.
Did Kimbo Kemble kick the kinsman's kettle?
If Kimbo Kemble kicked his kinsman's kettle.
Where's the kinsman's kettle Kimbo Kemble kicked?

☆   ☆   ☆

Knott was not in.
Knott was out
Knotting knots in netting.
Knott was out,
But lots of knots
Were in Knott's knotty netting.

Lame lambs limp.

☆   ☆   ☆

Languorous Lillie Lill looked
Lugubriously at the lowering clouds
And longed for lighter nights.

☆   ☆   ☆

Lanky Lawrence lost his lass and lobster.

☆   ☆   ☆

Last year I could not hear with either ear.

☆   ☆   ☆

Lazy Lionel Lippet loves lovely Lucy Locket.

☆   ☆   ☆

Lemon liniment.

☆   ☆   ☆

Lesser leather never weathered lesser wetter
weather.

☆   ☆   ☆

Let Lionel Lion lie on the lounger.

Lean
Linny
Long
loves
long
Lenny
Lean.

☆   ☆   ☆

Lester Liversidge and Liverpudlian loved litigation and learned the legal rules of the law.

☆   ☆   ☆

Let little Nellie run a little longer, Lottie.

☆   ☆   ☆

Lettice's limp lettuces.

☆   ☆   ☆

Let us go together to gather lettuce, whether the weather will let us or no.

☆   ☆   ☆   .

Libby Lobster loves cute Quentin Quail.

☆   ☆   ☆

Lily's lovely lolly cost a lot of Lily's lovely lolly!

☆   ☆   ☆

Literally literary literature in lots of libraries.

Little Boy Blue a big blue bubble blew.

☆ ☆ ☆

Little Willie' wooden whistle wouldn't whistle.

☆ ☆ ☆

Loathsome Lottie laughed less at Lillie's lilo than at Lulu's loofa.

☆ ☆ ☆

Look at the pug tugging at the rug.

☆ ☆ ☆

Loopy Lottie Lonnie—Dolly loves licking lovely lollies.

☆ ☆ ☆

Loopy Lulu looped eleven loops on the hoop-la hoop stall.

☆ ☆ ☆

Lots of little London lamplighters light London's lot of little lamps.

☆ ☆ ☆

Lovely lilaces line Lee's lonely lane.

☆ ☆ ☆

Lucy lingered, looking longingly for her lapdog.

Lucky Lillie likes to lighten her load when her load isn't too heavy to lighten.

☆   ☆   ☆

Lulu likes lemon lollies least.

☆   ☆   ☆

Madcap Michael made mincemeat out of mustard, marshmallows, and mulberries.

☆   ☆   ☆

Maggie Nanning, Maggie Nanning, Maggie Nanning.

☆   ☆   ☆

Malaria is a malady many men meet when meeting mosquitoes in Malaysia.

☆   ☆   ☆

Malicious Melissa maliciously maligned Millicent.

☆   ☆   ☆

'Manners maketh man', mocked Mark.

☆   ☆   ☆

Many an anemone sees an enemy anemone.

Many Mau-Mau meandered among the marshes, looking for missing missionaries.

☆   ☆   ☆

Many merry moments made many Misses mischievous.

☆   ☆   ☆

Many million mini-minors merrily milling around Milthorpe.

☆   ☆   ☆

Many millions must wish Micky and Minnie Mouse would marry in March.

☆   ☆   ☆

Marmalade and melon muesli.

☆   ☆   ☆

Many mincing maidens meandered moodily moorwards.

☆   ☆   ☆

Margaret and Monica Moore marched madly through monsoons,
Meeting many morons and taking many moons.

☆   ☆   ☆

Married name. Maiden name.

Master Maston must miss his mascot the mastiff.

☆   ☆   ☆

Maybe baby bees bounce in baby buggy buggies.

☆   ☆   ☆

Meek Morris Morrison made weak Matthew Matthews many milkshakes.

☆   ☆   ☆

Meek Margaret Mogel Mumbled magic messages.

☆   ☆   ☆

Meeny, Miney, Mooney and Mo
Meandered abroad when the wind did blow.
They wandered and wondered and wanted to know.
Whether the weather would turn to snow.

☆   ☆   ☆

Merry mermaids murmer mainly in the main.

☆   ☆   ☆

Messy May Messant may, but musing Maisie May mustn't.

☆   ☆   ☆

Midget Michael Merrymore was more merry than Cherry Bridget Moore.

Mild Madge misjudged Maggie's midget mascot.

☆   ☆   ☆

Milly Micklethwaite met a man minding a monkey for a millionaire.

☆   ☆   ☆

Milly Muscle suffered measles having sampled mussells.

☆   ☆   ☆

Miranda makes marvellous marshmallows that melt in the mouth.

☆   ☆   ☆

Miriam at the minaret mused among the mimosa in the moonlight.

☆   ☆   ☆

Miserable Manuel marched madly to meet Mabel Moss.

☆   ☆   ☆

Miserable Martha mumbles madly.

☆   ☆   ☆

Miss and Master Mouse gave Mrs. Mouse mouth-to-mouth resuscitation, so they were mouse-to-mouse.

☆   ☆   ☆

Miss Ruth's red roof thatch.

Miss Macintyre's tiresome tyre on her tricycle's twisted.

☆   ☆   ☆

Miss Maggie MacGregor makes magnificent macaroons.

☆   ☆   ☆

Miss Misty, Morris misses Mr. and Mrs. Morris mistletoe.

☆   ☆   ☆

Mix Maud more mud Mildred to make muddier mud pies.

☆   ☆   ☆

Mixed biscuits.

☆   ☆   ☆

Mixed metaphors muddle middling minds.

☆   ☆   ☆

Moaning Mona moaned unharmoniously.

☆   ☆   ☆

Monday lunchtime: Lundi Munchtime.

☆   ☆   ☆

'Mortars may not match my magic,' muttered the magician menacingly.

Mortimer, the mess steward, made a mish-mash of the mushrooms and murdered the mulligatawny.

☆　　☆　　☆

Mozart's music's madly melodious.

☆　　☆　　☆

Mr. Miller mills merrily with a miller's millstone.

☆　　☆　　☆

Moses supposes his toeses are roses;
But Moses supposes erroneously:
Because nobody's toeses
Are posies of roses,
As Moses supposes his toeses to be.

☆　　☆　　☆

Mr. Hadden had on his new Homburg hat but Mrs. Hadden hadn't a hat and after adding her money which was inadequate she had to adapt her old hat.

☆　　☆　　☆

Mr. Matthew Mathers, my maths master, munches mashed marmalade muffins.

☆　　☆　　☆

Mr. Mrs, Master and Miss Moth met
Miss, Master, Mrs and Mr. Moss.

Mr. See owned a saw
And Mr. Soar owned a seesaw.
Now See's saw soared Soar's seesaw
Before Sore saw See
Which made Soar sore,
Had Soar seen See's saw
Before See sawed Soar's seesaw
See's saw would not have sawed
Soar's seesaw.
So See's saw sawed Soar's seesaw.
But it was a shame to see Soar so sore
Just because See's saw sawed
Soar's seesaw.

☆   ☆   ☆

Mrs. Biggar had a baby, Which was the bigger?
The baby we know was a little Biggar,
But what of Mr. Biggar who was a father
Biggar?
However, Mr. Biggar died, was the baby then
bigger than Mrs. Bigger?
No the baby was not bigger. Why?
Because the baby had become fatherless.

☆   ☆   ☆

Mrs. Cripp's cat crept into the crypt, crept
around and crept out through a crack.

☆   ☆   ☆

Mrs. Lister's sister spoke Spanish, Swedish and
Swahill and spent a season in the Sudan where
she suffered from sunstroke.

Mrs. Marx marked Mark's mark card with a mark of merit.

☆　　☆　　☆

Mrs. Pipple-popple popped a pebble in poor Polly Pepper's eye.

☆　　☆　　☆

Mrs. Snelling selling six sick six-shilling sheep.

☆　　☆　　☆

Mumbling bumblings. Bumbling mumblings.

☆　　☆　　☆

Mushy mouthfuls of mushy mash.

☆　　☆　　☆

Must mussells have muscles?

☆　　☆　　☆

My dame hath a lame tame crane,
My dame hath a crane that is lame.
Pray gentle Jane, let my dame's tame crane
Feed and come home again.

☆　　☆　　☆

My master said 'that' is the right 'that' in that particular place.

☆　　☆　　☆

My wife gave Mr. Snipe's wife a swipe.

My mother made Mary, Minnie and Molly march many times round the room to martial music.

☆   ☆   ☆

My mother makes mince-meat mousse on Monday morning.

☆   ☆   ☆

My Miss Smith lisps and lists. She lisps as she talks and she lists as she walks.

☆   ☆   ☆

Nat's black bat's back on the mat.

☆   ☆   ☆

Naughty Nigel knotted tearful Tina's tights tightly in a knot.

Naughty Nelly's knitting knotted nighties for the navy.

☆   ☆   ☆

Naughty Nigel nearly knocked Norah needlessly.

☆   ☆   ☆

Ned needed to name no new names.

☆　　☆　　☆

Ned Nott was shot
And Sam Shott was not.
So it is better to be Shot than Nott.
Some say Nott was not shot.
But Shott says
He shot Nott.
Either the shot Shott shot at Nott
Was not shot, or
Nott was shot,
If the shot Shott shot shot Shott, then Shott
was shot,
Not Nott.
However,
The shot Shott shot shot not Shott— but Nott.

☆　　☆　　☆

Neddy Noodle nipped his neighbour's nutmegs.
Did Needy Noodle nip his neighbour's nutmegs?
If Needy Noodle nipped his neighbour's nutmegs,
Where are the nutmegs Needy Noodle nipped?

☆　　☆　　☆

Nice nieces nestle nicely in Nice.

☆　　☆　　☆

'Night, night, knight,' said one Knight to the
other Knight the other night. 'Night, night,
Knight.

☆　　☆　　☆

Nine numb ninnies notice nine dumb nannies.

Nina needs nine knitting needles to knit naughty
Nita's knickers nicely.

☆   ☆   ☆

Nine naughty nanny-goats nibble ninety-nine
nice new nasturtiums.

☆   ☆   ☆

Ninety-nine naughty knitted knick-knacks were
nicked by ninety-nine naughty knitted knick-
knack knickers.

☆   ☆   ☆

Nobby knew Noddy better than Noddy knew
Nobby.

☆   ☆   ☆

Norah needs lock-knit knickers.

☆   ☆   ☆

Now a sleeping car's known as a sleeper,
And sleepers for sleepers they keep,
And sleepers run under the sleepers
In which those sleepy sleepers sleep.

☆   ☆   ☆

Nana now knows whose knew banana was
given to Anna.

☆   ☆   ☆

Oh, don't groan at gentleman Gyles, the jolly jester.

☆   ☆   ☆

'Oh Horace, ain't it horrid when you're hot and in a hurry and you have to hold your hat on with your hand.'

☆   ☆   ☆

Old Dunn,
Young Dunn,
And Old Dunn's son.

☆   ☆   ☆

Once upon a barren moor,
There dwelt a bear, also a boar.
The bear could not bear the boar,
The boar thought the bear a bore.
At last the bear could bear no more
That boar that bored him on the moor.
And so one morn he bored the boar—
That boar will bore the bear no more!

☆   ☆   ☆

Old oily Olly oils old oily autos.

☆   ☆   ☆

Oliver Oglethorpe ogled an owl and an oyster.

Olive oil ointment.

☆   ☆   ☆

Once a feller met a feller
In a field of fitches,
Said a feller to a feller,
'Can a feller tell a feller,
Where a feller itches?'

☆   ☆   ☆

On the beach I see six small seals.

☆   ☆   ☆

Once I heard a mother utter,
'Daughter, go and shut the shutter.'
'Shutter's shut', the daughter uttered,
'For I can't shut it any shutter.'

☆   ☆   ☆

One fellow, he felt smart.
Two smart fellows, they felt smart.
Three smart fellows, they all felt smart.

☆   ☆   ☆

One hundred air-inhaling elephants.

☆   ☆   ☆

One old Ox opening oysters.

☆   ☆   ☆

Oporto, a port in Portugal, exports port.

One violet winkle veering west via Worthing went wading round Ventnor.

☆　　☆　　☆

Orange porridge.

☆　　☆　　☆

Oscar Owl howls hauntingly.

☆　　☆　　☆

Oswald Owl occupies the ancient old Oak.

☆　　☆　　☆

Oswald Whittle's whistle outwhistles all other whistler's whistles in Oswaldtwistle.

☆　　☆　　☆

Our black bull bled black blood on our blackthorn flower.

☆　　☆　　☆

Our great-grand-gran is a greater great-grand-gran than your great-grand-gran is.

☆　　☆　　☆

Our Joe wants to know if your Joe will lend our Joe your Joe's banjo. If your Joe won't lend our Joe your Joe's banjo, our Joe won't lend your Joe our Joe's banjo when our Joe has a banjo!

Outrageous Retta ran riot around Romford roundabouts.

☆   ☆   ☆

Outrageous Olive eats eight oranges hourly.

☆   ☆   ☆

Peggy Babcock, Peggy Babcock, Peggy Babcock.

☆   ☆   ☆

Peggy Pringle's posture at the piano was painful and practically impossible when she practised on the piccolo.

☆   ☆   ☆

Peppercorn pudding and pelican pie.

☆   ☆   ☆

Percy Poppled played the pipes
So prettily he tooted
But presently his lips were sore
So Percy's toots were muted.

☆   ☆   ☆

Perky Peter Perkins polished paper plates and plaster plaques for pleasure.

Perky Polly planted pretty precious pot plants.

★ ★ ★

Pete's Pa, Pete, poked at the pea patch to pick
a peck of peas for the poor pink pig in the pine
hole pig pen.

★ ★ ★

Peter Palmer painted a paper peacock, purple,
pink and puce.

★ ★ ★

Peter piles pink pails on pewter pots.

★ ★ ★

Peter Piper picked a pack of peppered Peanuts
to pickle.
If Peter Piper pickled a pack of peppered
peanuts,
Where are the pickled peppered peanuts Peter
Piper pickled?

★ ★ ★

Peter Piper picked a peck of pickled peppers.
Did Peter Piper pick a peck of pickled peppers?
If Peter Piper picked a peck of pickled peppers,
Where's the peck of pickled peppers Peter Piper
picked?

★ ★ ★

Peter Pringle printed press paragraphs.

Pheasant shooters had a pleasant shoot.

☆   ☆   ☆

Phone Phyllis to ask how fresh fish is, Phil.

☆   ☆   ☆

Pick up the picked plums please Peter.

☆   ☆   ☆

Pink peas please plump porkers.

☆   ☆   ☆

Pink primroses. Primrose pinks.

☆   ☆   ☆

Pink silk socks with shot silk spots.

☆   ☆   ☆

Pink spotted potato puddings.

☆   ☆   ☆

Pitter-patter
pitter-patter,
rather than
patter-pitter
patter-pitter.

☆   ☆   ☆

Plain plump Penelope played picquet pleasantly.

'Please cook crooked crabs, Cook.'

☆ ☆ ☆

Please, Paul, pause for applause.

☆ ☆ ☆

Please prepare Sir Percy for the Prime Minister's ministerial meeting.

☆ ☆ ☆

Plenty of Poltergeists prance around Pitlochry.

☆ ☆ ☆

Plenty of potatoes and tapioca pudding make people plump and pale.

☆ ☆ ☆

Podgy Paula Postlethwaite pockets pies and pasties.

☆ ☆ ☆

Polly Cox ate eight hollyhocks and now that eight-hollyhocks-eating Ox lies in a great mahogany box. Poor Polly Cox! Poor Ox!

☆ ☆ ☆

Poor Peter's poodle was pulled out of a puddle by a paddle.

☆ ☆ ☆

Pragmatic politicians pontificate precociously.

Precocious porcupines plod painfully through the pickles.

☆   ☆   ☆

Pretty Pamela Parker picked pink petunia posies.

☆   ☆   ☆

Pretty Pansy Parker parked her pram in people's pantries.

☆   ☆   ☆

Pretty pink pyjama patterns.

☆   ☆   ☆

Pretty posies prancing proudly.

☆   ☆   ☆

Pretty Priscilla presses pillow-slips.

☆   ☆   ☆

Pre-shrunk shirts for thrifty shoppers.

☆   ☆   ☆

Proud Percival pestered the Pastor for a promised prayer.

☆   ☆   ☆

'Pucker, Pearl Potter, please,'
Pleaded Pete Perkins politely.

☆   ☆   ☆

Pure food for four pure mules.

☆ ☆ ☆

Put Percy's presents in the post at present, Patience.

☆ ☆ ☆

Put the cut pumpkin in a pipkin.

☆ ☆ ☆

Quick kiss! Quicker kiss! Quickest kiss!

☆ ☆ ☆

Quick quiet quarrels.

☆ ☆ ☆

Quick quiet quills quote Queeny's quarrels.

☆ ☆ ☆

Quick, whitewash wicket quite white.

☆ ☆ ☆

Quinine quickly quells the quaking and cools the quesay quivers.

Quinn's twin sisters sing tongue twisters.

☆   ☆   ☆

Quixote Quicksight quizzed a queerish quidbox.
Did Quixote Quicksight quiz a queerish quidbox?
If Quixote Quicksight quizzed a queerish quidbox,
Where's the queerish quidbox Quixote Quicksight
quizzed?

☆   ☆   ☆

Ranjit, the runner from Rangoon, ran round the
ramparts during Ramadan.

☆   ☆   ☆

Rapidly Red read what Ned wrote in red water
colour.

☆   ☆   ☆

Rascally ruffians robbed the Regent.

☆   ☆   ☆

Reading bells ring rapidly as reeds rustle round
rivers.

☆   ☆   ☆

Real red rose rosettes.

Red leather!
Yellow leather!

☆ ☆ ☆

Red lorry, yellow lorry.

☆ ☆ ☆

Red roses rustle rurally.

☆ ☆ ☆

Red rubies round ring.

☆ ☆ ☆

Reds rule. Blue rules.

☆ ☆ ☆

Richard gave Robin a rap in the ribs for roasting the rabbit so rare.

☆ ☆ ☆

Rimsky-Korsakov really composed cracking compositions, of course.

☆ ☆ ☆

Riotous Ruby runs rings around Rubic's cubes.

☆ ☆ ☆

Riotous Ricky Wiley really wrote Rocking Robin rottenly.

Rita Rabbit robbed Retta Rabbit recently, ruining Retta's warren.

☆   ☆   ☆

Rita relishes Russian radishes.

☆   ☆   ☆

Roads close, so snow slows shows.

☆   ☆   ☆

Robin Redbreast's bad breath.

☆   ☆   ☆

Robin Robson was robbing Dobbin Dobson and was nabbed by Dobbin's godson.

☆   ☆   ☆

Rotten writing is written rotten.

☆   ☆   ☆

Rory Rumpus rode a rawboned racer.
Did Rory Rumpus ride a rawboned racer?
If Rory Rumpus rode a rawboned racer,
Where's the rawboned racer Rory Rumpus rode?

☆   ☆   ☆

Round the rugged rocks the ragged rascal ran.

☆   ☆   ☆

Rubber baby-buggy bumpers.

Sad Cinderella cried sweeping cinders.

☆　　☆　　☆

Sad Sam Smither's in a dither about Sid Withers.

☆　　☆　　☆

'Sally's solly,' said Silly Sa-si from Siam.

☆　　☆　　☆

Sally Wally dilly dallies daily.

☆　　☆　　☆

Sammy sitting singing
Sought Suzie Shaw,
Since Suzie started sobbing,
Sammy's stopped seeking.

☆　　☆　　☆

Sarah saw a sash shop full of showy, shiny sashes.

☆　　☆　　☆

Sarah Snifter sneezes sniffily.

☆　　☆　　☆

Saucy Sally saw silly Sam sewing sunflower seeds and sobbing simultaneously.

Say this sharply, say this sweetly,
Say this shortly, say this softly,
Say this sixteen times in succession.

☆   ☆   ☆

Send ten tonnes of pink tinted toilet tissue to
Tim Timms of Taunton.

☆   ☆   ☆

Seth hoes Beth's rows.

☆   ☆   ☆

Seven level streets with several level crossings.

☆   ☆   ☆

Seven Severn salmon swallowing seven Severn
shrimps.

☆   ☆   ☆

Seven shaggy sheepdogs shook sand
everywhere.

☆   ☆   ☆

Seventeen slimy slugs in satin sunbonnets sat
singing short sad songs.

☆   ☆   ☆

Seventy shuddering sailors stood silent as short
sharp shattering shocks shook the splendid
ship.

Shadows shade the sheltered shallows.

☆   ☆   ☆

Shakespeare's sonnets show simple passion.

☆   ☆   ☆

Shall chef chop chopped meat chipolatas or chop chipped beef chips instead?

☆   ☆   ☆

Shall Sarah Silling share her silver shilling?

☆   ☆   ☆

Shall Shadd and Cheri see several sailing ships on Chautauqua's shores?

☆   ☆   ☆

Shall Sheila show several sailors sheets that she has sewn?

☆   ☆   ☆

Sharon shook Aaron's hair on a Baron's air.

☆   ☆   ☆

Shave a cedar shingle thin.

☆   ☆   ☆

She chews cream cheese and fresh cress sandwiches.

She said she should show the shrewd shrew
the same shoe she threw the shrewd shrew.

☆   ☆   ☆

She said she suffered a short sharp shock,
Sean.

☆   ☆   ☆

She sat in solitude and isolation sighing and
singing sad songs.

☆   ☆   ☆

She saw several swift sloops swing shorewards
before she saw spaceships soar.

☆   ☆   ☆

She saw shiny soap suds sailing down the
shallow sink.

☆   ☆   ☆

She says she shall sew a sheet.

☆   ☆   ☆

She was a thistle-sifter
And she sifted thistles.
She had a sieveful of sifted thistles,
And a sieveful of unsifted thistles.
The sieveful of unsifted thistles
She had to sift
She was a thistle-sifter.

She sells seashells on the seashore, but she sells seashells, sherry and sandshoes on the seashore.

☆　　☆　　☆

She stops at the shops where I shop,
And if she shops at the shops where I shop
I won't shop at the shop where she shops!

☆　　☆　　☆

She stood on the balcony inexplicably mimicking him hiccuping and welcoming him in!

☆　　☆　　☆

Shears have sharp shining points.

☆　　☆　　☆

Sheared sheep shouldn't sleep in shacks.
Sheared sheep should sleep in sheds.

☆　　☆　　☆

'Sheath thy sword,' the surly Sheriff said. 'Or surely shall a churlish serf soon shatter thee.'

☆　　☆　　☆

Sheep shouldn't sleep in shaky shacks, should they?

☆　　☆　　☆

Sheila sewed shirts seriously.

Sheila's shetland pony shied, shocked Sheila's stupified.

☆   ☆   ☆

She stood at the door of Burgess's fish-sauce shop welcoming him in.

☆   ☆   ☆

Ships lie shattered on the shingle.

☆   ☆   ☆

Ships slip to shore.

☆   ☆   ☆

Shipshape suit shops ship shapely suits.

☆   ☆   ☆

Shirley Bassey shakes big unsuspecting spenders.

☆   ☆   ☆

Shirley slid the shears down the slippery slanting slates.

☆   ☆   ☆

Short sweet sausage meat.

☆   ☆   ☆

Should Sarah show Sally some shiny shoes or silk socks instead?

Should Sheena shout 'Sheila', or should Sheila shout 'Sheena'?

☆   ☆   ☆

Should Sheila shun sunshine, Celia?

☆   ☆   ☆

Shy Sam Smith thought Sarah Short so sweet.

☆   ☆   ☆

Shy Sarah saw six Swiss wrist watches.

☆   ☆   ☆

Shy Sheila shocked sister Suzie as she shouted shocking sayings.

☆   ☆   ☆

Shy Suzie Simpson sewed the seams securely side by side.

☆   ☆   ☆

Shy sly Sheila sat shivering in her slim, shiny short silk socks.

☆   ☆   ☆

Sidney Shelley thrust six thick sticks through sixty-six ricks.

☆   ☆   ☆

Silver thimbles.
Silver thimbles.

Silly Sally's silky shoes and soppy socks.

☆　　☆　　☆

Silly Sammy Stokes spilt some sticky syrup on the stove.

☆　　☆　　☆

Simon and Steven slept blissfully and securely side by side.

☆　　☆　　☆

Sing songs sung sadly Sammy.

☆　　☆　　☆

Simon Short-Smithfield's Sole Surviving Shoemaker Shoes Soles- Sewed Super-finely.

☆　　☆　　☆

Simple Simon swallowed several socks to soak up cider.

☆　　☆　　☆

Sinful Caesar sipped his snifter, seized his knees and sneezed.

☆　　☆　　☆

Sinister silent shapes shock several soldiers on the seashore.

☆　　☆　　☆

Sister Sally sewed silver socks with silver stitches.

☆ ☆ ☆

Sister Sandy sneezes slightly slicing succulent shallots.

☆ ☆ ☆

Sister Sarah sang seventy-six songs several Sundays running.
If sister Sarah sang seventy-six songs several Sundays running,
What were the seventy-six songs sister Sarah sang, Susan?

☆ ☆ ☆

Six long slim slick slender saplings.

☆ ☆ ☆

Six sausages shimmering on a shop counter.

☆ ☆ ☆

Six savoury sausages sizzling.

☆ ☆ ☆

Six Scots soldiers shooting snipe.

☆ ☆ ☆

Six sick city slickers sit.

☆ ☆ ☆

Six Sicilian snakes sibilantly sang six silly serenades to six Serbian serpents.

☆   ☆   ☆

Six silly sisters sell silk to six sickly senior citizens.

☆   ☆   ☆

Six skyscrapers stood snugly side by side shimmering beside the seaside.

☆   ☆   ☆

Six Swiss ships swiftly shift.

☆   ☆   ☆

Sixty-seven sacks of salt sitting side by side.

☆   ☆   ☆

Sixty-seven senior citizens sitting on a seat.

☆   ☆   ☆

Sixty-six shy shepherds serenely sailing a ship at sea.

☆   ☆   ☆

Slapped slimey slush shivers slightly.

☆   ☆   ☆

Slim Sam shaved six slippery chinas in sixty-six seconds.

Slim Sam slid sideways on the slope.

☆　　☆　　☆

Slim satellites sending scintillating signals.

☆　　☆　　☆

Sly Sid slid slyly sideways.

☆　　☆　　☆

Sly Stevie said sleep walking was solely the somnambulists concern.

☆　　☆　　☆

Snoodles ship snuff for shops.

☆　　☆　　☆

Snow slight: no snipe.

☆　　☆　　☆

Softly, silently, the scythe
Slithered through the thick sweet sward;
Seething, sweating, sad serfs writhe,
Slicing swathes so straight and broad.

☆　　☆　　☆

Soldiers' shoulders shudder when shrill shells shriek.

☆　　☆　　☆

Some say sweet-scented shaving soap soothes sore skins.

Some shun sunshine.

☆   ☆   ☆

Something whistled past my head.
'I missed again!' my Mrs. said.

☆   ☆   ☆

Some think Tom Thumb's plumb dumb.

☆   ☆   ☆

Stan slid in his sled and slithered to a stop.

☆   ☆   ☆

Steady Stan! Stand steady.

☆   ☆   ☆

Steady stallions stride strongly.

☆   ☆   ☆

Steer clear of scythes, shears, scissors and
sharp steel spears, shun stalactites and
stalagmites, stagnant pools, stale sausages,
scorpions and stag beetles.

☆   ☆   ☆

'Stick several sellotape strips, not string,' she
said.

☆   ☆   ☆

Stop Chop Shops selling Chop Shop chops!

Strange strategic statistics.

☆   ☆   ☆

Strikes strangle struggle, squandering scheduled synthesis.

☆   ☆   ☆

Students study stencilling steadily.

☆   ☆   ☆

Stunning Estella stunned Stanley with astonishment.

☆   ☆   ☆

Stupid Stella Stubbins stifled Stephen Stubbing.

☆   ☆   ☆

Sulky Suki sucked sugar and sherbert through straws.

☆   ☆   ☆

Sunshine Susie shone her shoes with soap and shoe-shine.

☆   ☆   ☆

Suppose Sally shredded suet so swiftly that she was sooner done than she expected.
How slowly would Sally have to shred suet to be done as soon as she expected she would be?

'Surely Sylvia swims!' shrieked Sammy, surprised, 'Somebody should show Sylvia some strokes so she shall not sink!'

☆   ☆   ☆

Susan Schumann shot a solitary chamois and received a sharp salutary shock from such shameless slaughter.

☆   ☆   ☆

Swan, swim over the sea.
Swim, swan, swim!
Swan, swim back again!
Well swum, swan.

☆   ☆   ☆

Swedish sword swallowers shift short swords swiftly.

☆   ☆   ☆

Sweet Sheila Shoxtock sells sugar shakers to Sheiks.

☆   ☆   ☆

Swim, Sam, swim,
Show them you're a swimmer!
Six sharp sharks are out to take your liver,
So swim, Sam, swim!

☆   ☆   ☆

Ten tame tadpoles tucked tightly together in a tall thin tin.

☆   ☆   ☆

Ten tiny toddling tots trying to train their tongues to trill.

☆   ☆   ☆

Ten tiny tortoises talk to twenty timid toads.

☆   ☆   ☆

Ten thatchers went to thatch ten tiny thatched cottages, taking ten tight bundles of thatching straw with them to thatch with.

☆   ☆   ☆

Thadeus sang his thrilling song for the theatrical songsters.

☆   ☆   ☆

That bloke's back brake-block broke.

☆   ☆   ☆

The aboriginal bush-ranger became a brigand and battened on the poor bush beasts.

☆   ☆   ☆

The bailiff brought the birds for breakfast.

The accountant cut along to the counting house-out of countenance as his cash didn't tally with his careful calculations.

☆ ☆ ☆

The Archbishop's cat crept craftily into Canterbury Cathedral crypt causing cataclysmal chaos in clerical circles by keeping cunningly concealed.

☆ ☆ ☆

The author put his autograph in the hectograph together with his photograph and sent a copy with *The Daily Telegraph* to his grandma in Arkansas.

☆ ☆ ☆

The bad lad limps gladly along the badly-lighted landing.

☆ ☆ ☆

The best blowing bugler in the Boston brass band.

☆ ☆ ☆

The big black-backed bumblebee.

☆ ☆ ☆

The bleak breeze blights the bright bloom blossom.

☆ ☆ ☆

The bottle of perfume that Willie sent was highly displeasing to Millicent.
Her thanks were so cold, they quarrelled, I'm told, through that silly scent Willie sent Millicent.

☆　　☆　　☆

The broom blooms when the bluebell blooms.

☆　　☆　　☆

'The bun is better buttered,' Billy muttered.

☆　　☆　　☆

The brown cows in Cowes chew more cud than the white cows in Cowes.
There are more brown cows in Cowes than white cows in Cowes.

☆　　☆　　☆

The busy bee buzzed busily around the busy beehive.

☆　　☆　　☆

The cat-catchers can't catch caught cats.

☆　　☆　　☆

The chased treasure chest's thrice chipped.

☆　　☆　　☆

The cheeky Czech choked on a chunk of chocolate as he chattered cheerily to Charlie the chimp.

The chief constable concentrated on combing the area around Castlewich where the crooked criminals had committed the crime.

☆   ☆   ☆

The conundrum constructed by the communist was catastrophical.

☆   ☆   ☆

The cox crew rowed at cock's crow.

☆   ☆   ☆

The crazy cockroach crowned the crooked cricket.

☆   ☆   ☆

The cruel ghoul's cool gruel.

☆   ☆   ☆

The crew unscrewed the screws and clipped the sheet to the clews.

☆   ☆   ☆

The cringing crooner couldn't recall the tune and cried constantly.

☆   ☆   ☆

The crow flew over the river with a raw lump of liver.

The customs official whistled at the concealed contraband.

☆   ☆   ☆

The desperado designed the desperate plot to dupe the dreadful dramatist.

☆   ☆   ☆

The dim don dropped the drum.

☆   ☆   ☆

The diplodocus played hocus-pocus when he couldn't focus on a crocus.

☆   ☆   ☆

The dolphin swam dolorously and dolefully around the dolphinarium.

☆   ☆   ☆

The dragnet dragged deliberately downstream and discovered the drowned duke.

☆   ☆   ☆

The drain in the train dripped again and again, until the drain in the train dripped dry.

☆   ☆   ☆

The duchess danced gracefully and daintily and drew delightful glances.

The dude dropped in at the Dewdrop Inn for a drop to drink.

☆   ☆   ☆

The dustman daily does his duty to dislodge the dirty dust deposited in disgusting dusty dustbins.

☆   ☆   ☆

The faun faltered near the fortifications afraid of the thunder.

☆   ☆   ☆

The first fast master passed faster than the last just pastor.

☆   ☆   ☆

The flyer furled the flaring flag and flung it firmly from the fuselage.

☆   ☆   ☆

The frozen fishermen threw their fish back in again.

☆   ☆   ☆

The glow-worm's gleam glitters in glade and glen.

☆   ☆   ☆

The goats gravitated to the grazing ground and gravely gathered grass.

The grave games-man groused when the greyhound growled.

☆   ☆   ☆

The grotto underground was guarded at the gates by a glowing-eyed guard-dog.

☆   ☆   ☆

The gun glue grew glum.

☆   ☆   ☆

The hare's ears heard ere the hares heeded.

☆   ☆   ☆

The Hebrew blew the bugle lugubriously.

☆   ☆   ☆

The hedge hindered the homicide from hurting himself.

☆   ☆   ☆

The heir's hair gets into the heir's ear here.

☆   ☆   ☆

The heiress found the heirloom haphazardly hanging from the high shelf.

☆   ☆   ☆

The horse's hard hooves hit the hard high road.

☆   ☆   ☆

The host in Ulster uttered an oath,
What was the oath the Ulster host uttered?

☆ ☆ ☆

The interrogator incensed the interviewee with his incessant insistence on irrelevancies.

☆ ☆ ☆

Thelma Thistlethwaite saw thick thistles in the thatch.

☆ ☆ ☆

Thelma was thoroughly thankless.

☆ ☆ ☆

The lachrymose lamprey looked lingeringly at the limpet lolling on the rock.

☆ ☆ ☆

The Leith police dismisseth us.

☆ ☆ ☆

The librarian lent his literacy list to the Latin master to select eleven lessons.

☆ ☆ ☆

The lieutenant's lady loved liqueurs and liked to linger late with lots of creme-de-menthe.

☆ ☆ ☆

The lone leavers leave the leafy lane.

The man from Middlesborough misappro-priated money from the military mess and was remanded for a misdemeanour.

☆ ☆ ☆

The masts mask the majestic mansions and the multitudinous minarets.

☆ ☆ ☆

The mighty master murdered the maddened magistrate.

☆ ☆ ☆

The minx mixed a medical mixture.

☆ ☆ ☆

The Mohican was molested by a mulatto who mistook him for a Mohawk and mutilated his wigwam.

☆ ☆ ☆

The musician made music and moved multitudes.

☆ ☆ ☆

The myth of Miss Muffet.

☆ ☆ ☆

Then the thankless theologian thawed thoroughly.

☆ ☆ ☆

The new King's queen,
The new Queen's king.

☆   ☆   ☆

The new nuns knew the true nuns knew the new nuns too.

☆   ☆   ☆

Theophilus Twistle, less thrifty than some, thrust three thousand thistles through the thick of his thumb.

☆   ☆   ☆

The other mother's smothered in moss.

☆   ☆   ☆

The owner of the Inside Inn was outside his Inside Inn, with his inside outside his Inside Inn.

☆   ☆   ☆

The poor dog's paw poured water from every pore.

☆   ☆   ☆

The Pope poked a poker at the piper.
So the piper poked some pepper at the Pope.

☆   ☆   ☆

The postman placed the package at the postern and played peek-a-boo with Potter's poodle.

The rat-catchers can't catch caught rats.

☆   ☆   ☆

The prattling prig pranced around the prairie and played his ukelele to the priest.

☆   ☆   ☆

The quaint queen quickly quelled the quarrelsome quaker!

☆   ☆   ☆

The queue in the quadrangle at question-time was quite quiescent.

☆   ☆   ☆

The squirrel squeals with breathalysing indignation, quiveringly spluttering complete repudiation of the impossibly preposterous allegation of gross intoxication.

☆   ☆   ☆

The raucous corncrake created a querulous cacophony.

☆   ☆   ☆

The royal lady received the roses regally at the recent reception.

☆   ☆   ☆

The rushing river roars rudely round the regal Roman ruin.

Theresa tried on twenty-three silver thimbles.

☆   ☆   ☆

The religious relic reposed in the reliquary.

☆   ☆   ☆

There's the Mayor's mayoral mare.

☆   ☆   ☆

There are thirty thousand feathers on that thrush's throat.

☆   ☆   ☆

There was a buzz in the bazaar when the Arab from Arabia biffed the Berber from Beirut on the back of the bonce.

☆   ☆   ☆

There was an old lady from Ryde,
Who ate apple cider and died.
    The apples fermented
    Inside the lamented
And made cider inside her inside.

☆   ☆   ☆

There was an old lady called Carr,
Who took the 3.3 for Forfar;
    She said, I believe
    It's sure to leave
Before the 4.4 for Forfar.'

The saucy slippery scoundrel scampered scurrying by.

☆   ☆   ☆

The savour of the silly scent the sentry sent to Millicent.

☆   ☆   ☆

The scandal-monger uttered scurrilous statements until someone threatened to sue him for slander.

☆   ☆   ☆

The seething sea ceaseth seething.

☆   ☆   ☆

The sceptic questioned the schedule closely scrawled by the science master and seemed to suggest it should be scrapped.

☆   ☆   ☆

The school coal in the school coal scuttle was scattered by a cool scholar.

☆   ☆   ☆

The seething sea ceaseth and thus the seething sea sufficeth us.

☆   ☆   ☆

The sentinels cast sombre shadows over the Sahara desert.

The shepherds share the Shetland shawl.

☆   ☆   ☆

The short sort shoot straight through.

☆   ☆   ☆

The sick sixth Sheik's sixth sheep's sick.

☆   ☆   ☆

The sinking steamer sunk.

☆   ☆   ☆

The skunk sat on a stump and thunk the stump
    stunk
But the stump thunk the skunk stunk.

☆   ☆   ☆

The sleepless sleeper seeks sleep.

☆   ☆   ☆

The sloth loafs among the low slopes.

☆   ☆   ☆

The strenuous struggle seemed superfluous.

☆   ☆   ☆

The sordid slum sent shivers down her sensitive
spine.

☆   ☆   ☆

The strenuous struggle strangles the strong.

The strapping soldiers strived sternly to strengthen the stronghold.

☆ ☆ ☆

The suitability of a suet pudding without superfluous plums is a superstition presumably due to Susan's economy.

☆ ☆ ☆

The sultry siren stood and sulked in the sand dunes.

☆ ☆ ☆

The Sunday school sings spiritual songs spiritedly.

☆ ☆ ☆

The sun shines on shop signs.

☆ ☆ ☆

The sunshine sends shadow shows.

☆ ☆ ☆

The swan swims!
The swans swam!

☆ ☆ ☆

The swiftly swirling mill wheel grinds the gleaming corn.

☆ ☆ ☆

The threaded thimbles thrilled Thelma.

The tiresome wireless man's fireless
Whilst the fireless wirelessman's tireless.

☆   ☆   ☆

The tracker tracked and tricked and trapped
the tricky trickster.

☆   ☆   ☆

The troops tread the toilsome trail.

☆   ☆   ☆

The truants tramp trustingly towards Truro.

☆   ☆   ☆

The two-twenty tore through town.

☆   ☆   ☆

The winkle ship sank and the shrimp ship
swam.

☆   ☆   ☆

The wild wolf roams the wintry wastes.

☆   ☆   ☆

The wild wind whipped Walt from the wharf.

☆   ☆   ☆

The wire wound around a reel.

☆   ☆   ☆

The Wye wound right around the rye field.

☆   ☆   ☆

The yearly yield of yarn from Yarmouth is less than the total cocoa crop from Crewe.

☆   ☆   ☆

They thanked them thoroughly.

☆   ☆   ☆

They threw three thick things.

☆   ☆   ☆

They tried to tempt the tattered tramps to take the treacle tarts.

☆   ☆   ☆

Thin sticks; thick bricks.

☆   ☆   ☆

Thirty theatrical thespians threatened frolicsome theatre.

☆   ☆   ☆

Thirty thousand Thracians threatened Thessaly.

☆   ☆   ☆

Thirty thrifty farmers threw a fit.

☆   ☆   ☆

This crisp crust crackles crunchily.

Thirty thrifty whistling washers witchingly whistling, wishing washing was washed.

☆   ☆   ☆

This is a zither.

☆   ☆   ☆

This lute, with its flute-like tones, was captured in the loot of a great city, and its luminous sides are made of unpolluted silver.

☆   ☆   ☆

This myth is a mystery to me.

☆   ☆   ☆

Three blue beads in a blue bladder; rattle blue beads, rattle blue bladder.

☆   ☆   ☆

Three fiddling pigs sat in a pit and fiddled, Fiddle, piggy, fiddle, piggy, fiddle piggy.

☆   ☆   ☆

Three flee-flow pipes.

☆   ☆   ☆

Three grey green greedy geese,
Feeding on a weedy piece,
The piece was weedy,
And the geese were greedy,
Three grey green greedy geese.

Three grey geese crept into Clitheroe Castle.

☆ ☆ ☆

Three thick black plastic press blocks as previously supplied.

☆ ☆ ☆

Three Scotch thistles in the thicket.

☆ ☆ ☆

Three thrice-freed thieves threw thousands of thick thistles.

☆ ☆ ☆

Three thrushes thrilled them.

☆ ☆ ☆

Three thumping tigers tickling trout.

☆ ☆ ☆

Thrice times three, twice times two.

☆ ☆ ☆

Though a kiss be amiss,
She who misses the kisses,
As Miss without kiss,
May miss being Mrs.!

☆ ☆ ☆

Tim, the thin twin tinsmith.

Through six thick swamps stumbled Sammy.
Tie twine to three twigs.

☆   ☆   ☆

Timothy thanked Thomas Threlfall for his
thoughtfulness although
Father Threlfall had threatened him fearfully.

☆   ☆   ☆

Timothy Tiddles twiddled tightly twisted twine
ten times to test it.

☆   ☆   ☆

Timothy took Titus to Tavistock to teach the
tomtits to talk theology to the Turks that travel
through Tartary.

☆   ☆   ☆

Tiny orang-utan tongues.

☆   ☆   ☆

Tiny Tommy Tortoise talked to Tessie Turtle on
the telephone ten times today.

☆   ☆   ☆

Tiptoe Tommy turned a Turk for twopence.

☆   ☆   ☆

Tom Trapp's tip-top tom-tom.

☆   ☆   ☆

Tom turned to Ted.
Told Ted to try
To tie the tie
Tom tried to tie.

☆ ☆ ☆

Twelve tall tulips turning to the sun.

☆ ☆ ☆

Tommy Tickle tickled his teacher,
Where did Tommy Tickle's teacher tickle
Tommy?

☆ ☆ ☆

Tommy Turner turned away from the moral
turpitude and tried to teach the two virtues of
tolerance and tranquillity to his twins.

☆ ☆ ☆

Tommy Tye
Tried to tie his tie,
But tugging too tight
Tore his tie.

☆ ☆ ☆

Tonight is a light night,
So you mustn't light a night light
On a light night like this.

☆ ☆ ☆

Tony, try telling twenty thrilling tales to twenty
tiny tots.

To sit in solemn silence
In a dim dark dock
Awaiting the sensation
Of a short sharp shock
From a cheap and chippy chopper
On a big black block.

☆   ☆   ☆

Truly rural.

☆   ☆   ☆

Twine twisted twigs twenty twirls.

☆   ☆   ☆

Twenty tiny tots twisting through the turnstiles.

☆   ☆   ☆

Twenty tiny typewriters typed in tiny type.

☆   ☆   ☆

Twenty tinkers took two hundred tintacks to
Toy Town.
If twenty tinkers took two hundred tintacks to
Toy Town,
How many tintacks to Toy Town did each of
the twenty tinkers going to Toy Town take?

☆   ☆   ☆

Twenty-two thundering trains flashed through
thirty tunnels.

Two boot blacks, a white boot black and a black boot black, stood together doing nothing.

The white boot black proposed that he should black the boots of the black boot black.

The black boot black was perfectly willing to have his boots blacked by the white boot black.

So the white boot black began to black the boots of the black boot black.

But when the white boot black had blacked one boot of the black boot black,

He declined to black the other boot of the black boot black,

Until the black boot black had blacked both boots of the white boot black.

However, the black boot black refused point blank to black the boots of the white boot black, and said he didn't care whether the white boot black blacked the other boot black or not.

He considered that one boot blacked was enough for a black boot black, and that a black boot black with one boot blacked was better than a white boot black with no boots blacked.

Then the white boot black called the black boot black a black blackguard.

Of course, when the white boot black began blacking the character of the black boot black, the black boot black began blacking the face of the white boot black all black with the blacking on the boot the white boot black and blacked, and the white boot black blacked the black boot black back.

When the Society of Black and White Boot Blackers considered the matter, they characterised the conduct of both boot blacks as the blackest affair that had ever blackened the pages of boot-black history.

Two thirsty thatchers thoughtfully thatched a thrush's nest—such a thankless task.

☆   ☆   ☆

Two toads totally tired trying to trot to Tidsbury.

☆   ☆   ☆

Two tubby teddies toasting tasty teacakes.

☆   ☆   ☆

Two tugs toil Tynewards.

☆   ☆   ☆

Twisty twining twirling tendrils tethering together tightly ten tall trees.

☆   ☆   ☆

Twixt Trent and Tweed.

☆   ☆   ☆

Typical tropical trivial trite trash.

☆   ☆   ☆

Typing ten-times-tables takes more time than typing ten-times-two.

☆   ☆   ☆

Ted threw Fred three free throws.

☆   ☆   ☆

Unique New York.

★   ★   ★

United States twin-screw steel cruisers.

★   ★   ★

Unless the two tots titter, you'll tell the oft-told tale.

★   ★   ★

Urgent detergent.

★   ★   ★

Uriah Heep sounded servile, obsequious and smarmy.

★   ★   ★

Valiant vassels vexed Victoria.

★   ★   ★

Vera was very vulnerable and the vulgar verbosity of the volatile Venetians vitiated her vocabulary.

★   ★   ★

Vigorous Vesta voiced voluble verse vociferously.

☆   ☆   ☆

Vile Willy's wily violin.

☆   ☆   ☆

Viola valued the valley violets in Vera's vase.

☆   ☆   ☆

Villiam Veedom viped his vig and vaistcoat.
Did Villiam Veedom vipe his vig and vaistcoat?
If Villiam Veedom viped his vig and vaistcoat.
Where are the vig and vaistcoat
Villiam Veedom viped?

☆   ☆   ☆

Violet vainly viewed the vast, vacant vista.

☆   ☆   ☆

'Walter, get water from the waiter!'

☆   ☆   ☆

Walter Waddle won a wager. I wonder which wager Walter Waddle won?

☆   ☆   ☆

Walter Wooster worshipped Worcester Sauce.

Weak writers want white ruled writing paper.

☆ ☆ ☆

Weary Willie wheezed woozily the wrong way round.

☆ ☆ ☆

We eat what we can and what we can't, we can.

☆ ☆ ☆

We had a knocker-up, and our
knocker-up had a knocker-up, and our
knocker-up's knocker-up didn't knock
our knocker-up. So our knocker-up
didn't knock us up, 'cos he's not up!'

☆ ☆ ☆

Were the Waughs at war last year or are the Waughs at war here?

☆ ☆ ☆

We surely shall see the sun shine soon.

☆ ☆ ☆

What's here was there.
That's what was here.

☆ ☆ ☆

Wheedling, weeping Winnie wails wildly.

When all else fails, say 'Hail to all ales!'

☆   ☆   ☆

When a twiner a twisting will twist him a twist,
For the twining his twist he three times doth
untwist,
But if one of the twines of the twist do untwist,
The twine that untwisteth, untwisteth the twist;
Untwirling the twine that untwisteth between,
He twists with his twister the twain in a twine;
Then twice having twisted the twains in the
twine,
He twisteth the twines he had twisted in vain.
The twain that, in twisting before in the twine,
As twines were untwisted, he now doth untwine,
'Twixt the twain intertwisting a twine more
between,
He, twisting his twister, makes a twist of the
twine.

☆   ☆   ☆

When you want to wear your woollies and your
wellies wait till winter draws on.

☆   ☆   ☆

Which is the witch that wished the wicked
wish? I don't know which witch is which.

☆   ☆   ☆

'Which switch, miss, is the switch for Ipswich,
miss?'

Whistle for the thistle sifter.

☆　　☆　　☆

Who washed Washington's white woollen underwear when Washington's washerwoman went West?

☆　　☆　　☆

Who will wet the thetstone while Willy whistles wistfully?

☆　　☆　　☆

'Whose shoe?' sighed Sue.
'My shoes,' lied Lou.
'Here's your shoe, Lou,' cried Sue.
'Shucks, Sue, thank you,' Lou sighed.
'My shoe,' cried Blue, 'I'll sue Lou and Sue!'

☆　　☆　　☆

Wiles and snares and snares and wiles of a snary, wily world.

☆　　☆　　☆

Will he? Won't he, Willie?

☆　　☆　　☆

Will real wheels really wheel?

☆　　☆　　☆

Will Wilma want Will on Wednesday week, Willie?

Will Willie Wilkins be willing to wish Willis welcome words?

☆   ☆   ☆

Will Winnie wander with Will, or will Will wander with Winnie?
We wonder.

☆   ☆   ☆

Wise Wilma while weaving worsted waistcoats whistled wistfully.

☆   ☆   ☆

Wishy-washy wished to win a wager.

☆   ☆   ☆

With a shovel Sarah slowly shifted sifted cinders.

☆   ☆   ☆

Would Wendy wander when it's windy, Wanda?

☆   ☆   ☆

Would William White whisper 'from whence' and why?

☆   ☆   ☆

Would Willy Watson wander wearily round Regents Park, we wonder?

☆   ☆   ☆

Would Winnie wish to come a-wassailing?

☆   ☆   ☆

Yellow yo-yo's.

☆   ☆   ☆

You see yonder's Yorkshire's youngsters.

☆   ☆   ☆

You can have—
Fried fresh fish,
Fish fried fresh
Fresh fried fish,
Fresh fish fried,
Or fish fresh fried.

☆   ☆   ☆

You sent me your bill, Berry,
Before it was due, Berry.
Your father, the elder Berry,
Had not been such a goose, Berry.

☆   ☆   ☆

Your Bob owes our Bob a bob, and if your Bob doesn't give our Bob that bob your Bob owes our Bob, our Bob will give your Bob a bob on the bob!

☆   ☆   ☆

Young Dunn,
Will be Dunn,
When Old Dunn's done.

☆   ☆   ☆